"David Edwards is one of the best communicators I have ever heard. He knows the heartbeat of the culture. It is exciting for me to see what he has done with this awesome book. I want to encourage you to read this material and let others in on what God is doing through David."

— JEFF LOVINGOOD, next generation pastor; Long Hollow Baptist Church, Hendersonville, Tennessee

"David Edwards has combined the passion of an evangelist and the teaching of a scholar in this book. In a time when students are biblically illiterate, David has called out a generation of students who will authentically pursue the mission of God found in the pages of Scripture. Students are looking for something to give their lives away to, and the raw meat of the Word of God is exactly what they have been looking for."

— SPENCER BARNARD, pastor to students, East Side Baptist Church, Fort Smith, Arkansas

"What a great resource for helping students take in the Word and begin to live in it. First Book is the perfect name for these studies. The entire design makes *First Book Challenge* a great option for a small group of students as well as a great tool to build a weekend event around."

— RANDY HALL, CEO, Student Life

"Finally, a book that is radically committed to the Word of God and yet remains functionally practical. John Stamper brings his wealth of ministry experience to those who desire to follow the Lord Jesus Christ. John and David nail it in this book by presenting profound truth in a simplistic and action-oriented strategy."

— DR. DAVID E. ADAMS, executive director, International Center for Youth and Family Ministry, Southern Baptist Theological Seminary and Boyce College

"After serving the local church the past thirty-eight years as a student pastor, I have no doubt that what is needed most in the hearts and lives of this generation is the Word of God. Anything that can help a student connect or reconnect with the Word of God and His voice is worthy of my attention, time, and investment. *First Book Challenge* is powerful and effective, especially for such a time as this. It is the perfect resource for every teen, youth group, club, and home."

PHIL NEWBERRY, campus pastor, Bellevue Arlington, Arlington, Tennessee

"I've watched kids change the course of their culture and make a difference for Christ on their campus using the principles that John and Dave teach using *First Book Challenge*. As a parent, I've benefited from my teens using the First Book message and methods. As a pastor, I've watched a groundswell of a movement that has changed homes and families. I'm eager to see God use this resource to change a generation."

— DR. RICHARD MARK LEE, senior pastor, First Baptist Church,
McKinney, Texas

"David and John have made this simple for leaders of students. With *First Book Challenge*, not only are we creatively teaching the principles of God's Word in a unique way but we are also teaching students how to study the Scriptures for themselves. We plan to expose as many students as possible to this incredible new resource."

— GREG DAVIS, president, First Priority Ministry

"I've read the material, and all I can say is wow! There are books that impact a few lives, and then there are books like this one that alter churches, schools, cities, states, and nations! Dave Edwards has a track record of being a transformational author, and through *First Book Challenge*, he is at his best. Every student ministry in the country needs to take this journey."

— TONY NOLAN, speaker; author

"This is exactly what our students and adults need. Giving our students a handle to not only get in the Word but also get the Word in them is going to make an impact."

— MATTHEW CROWE, student pastor,
First Baptist Church Black Forest, Colorado Springs, Colorado

BOOST ///

FIRST BOOK CHALLENGE

EMPOWERED BY THE HOLY SPIRIT

DAVID EDWARDS • JOHN STAMPER

NAVPRESS
Discipleship Inside Out™

THINK

Discipleship Inside Out™

NavPress is the publishing ministry of The Navigators, an international Christian organization and leader in personal spiritual development. NavPress is committed to helping people grow spiritually and enjoy lives of meaning and hope through personal and group resources that are biblically rooted, culturally relevant, and highly practical.

For a free catalog go to www.NavPress.com
or call 1.800.366.7788 in the United States or 1.800.839.4769 in Canada.

ISBN-13: 978-1-61747-167-4

Cover design by Faceout Studio
Cover image by Shutterstock
Author photos by Travis Clancy Photography, Edmond, OK

Some of the anecdotal illustrations in this book are true to life and are included with the permission of the persons involved. All other illustrations are composites of real situations, and any resemblance to people living or dead is coincidental.

Unless otherwise identified, all Scripture quotations in this publication are taken from the *Holy Bible, New International Version*® (NIV®). Copyright © 1973, 1978, 1984 by International Bible Society. Used by permission of Zondervan. All rights reserved. The other version used is the New American Standard Bible® (NASB), Copyright © 1960, 1962, 1963, 1968, 1971, 1972, 1973, 1975, 1977, 1995 by The Lockman Foundation. Used by permission.

Printed in the United States of America

1 2 3 4 5 6 7 8 / 17 16 15 14 13 12

CONTENTS

FOREWORD

Can I feel God? Is there any way I can find an answer to my personal crises? What do I do about my relationships? These, along with many others, are questions that students are asking the church and the student ministry to answer. Sadly, the answers they hear from pulpits and platforms are often emotionally centered, not compelling, and lacking enough content and substance to make a difference in the way students answer the questions of life and deal with their drama. What results from this is students leave the church in search of better answers. Something crucial is missing.

The priority and the use of Scripture have almost disappeared for many. The Word of God is often no longer a part of church service and student night. It has been de-elevated. The tragic result is that students are trying to answer their questions, deal with their problems, and take on life without reliable truth. We have a generation of students whose identity is defined by whatever one needs it to be and wherever one happens to find it.

God never intended our lives to be lived this way. Scripture points us to a creative God of Truth and a loving Savior. The Bible can be trusted. I thank God for the First Book Challenge and what it will mean to students. In a culture where the Bible is readily available, the key is to present answers in a relevant way that grips the heart and mind. The First Book Challenge helps students know how to interact with Scripture and make God's Book their First Book.

The First Book Challenge is compelling. It teaches students how to not only understand God's Word but also live it out in relationships. The information in this three-book series is powerful and will impact the way people do life. One part of the First Book Challenge is that each student would receive a Bible to study as part of this series and then give it away to a friend who doesn't have one – that is good news! I believe that by getting students into the Word and the Word into the life of students, we can see a cultural change in the home, school, and church. I am thrilled for you and your student ministry to take the First Book Challenge!

JOSH MCDOWELL
writer, researcher, speaker

THE FIRST BOOK CHALLENGE

In those days the word of the LORD was rare.

1 SAMUEL 3:1

Samuel's world was wordless. The Word of God had been so devalued that it was not spoken, read, or heard. Tragically, the same is true about our world. We live in a quickly changing culture. Shifting values produce self-stylized spirituality and a search for self-fulfillment. It would be easy to assign the blame to music, art, entertainment, or government, but the truth is that a clear understanding of the importance of the Word of God has been removed from the landscape of society. We find ourselves living in a world of moral gray areas where the lines have been so blurred that it is difficult to tell right from wrong. This is evidenced by the rise of social drinking, the decline of moral boundaries, a loss of respect for others, a heightened sense of entitlement, and a driving belief that people are only a means to an end. Ironically, access to the Word of God is not the problem. Bibles fill the lost-and-found boxes in many churches. What *is* lacking is a personal connection to God's Word accompanied by skills to understand and use the Bible.

Without a working knowledge of Scripture, you will lose your grasp on God's Word. This releases a chain reaction of anger and resentment, which leads to lack of purpose and disappointment with life. Losing your grasp on God's Word and truth makes it more likely that you will steal, be abusive to others, cheat on an exam, use illegal drugs, attempt suicide, or participate in other physically, emotionally, or spiritually destructive behaviors. The Bible is the change agent for this generation. A deeply held belief in God and His Word will serve as the foundation of your faith so that no matter what comes your way, you can stand strong. God has always been speaking, even in Samuel's day. The Word of God still speaks. The question for us today is "Who is listening?"

There is a generation of students who refuse to listen to the prevailing voice of society and its relentless pursuit of materialism. They will no longer be led astray by easy "believe-ism" but instead have embraced God's standard of absolute truth and the pursuit of godliness. They have heard the call to continue holding on to the priority of Scripture, believing that the Word of God proclaims salvation for all. They believe the Bible is not a textbook but the very revelation of Christ, who is our hope for eternal life. The Bible uniquely unlocks the true identity, purpose, and destiny of our lives. It assures us that God has not left us alone to grope our way through life but has given us His wisdom in His Word to be studied, believed, and obeyed. This is a generation that is pursuing biblical faith, is rooted and grounded in God's Word, and speaks with conviction the truths of Scripture. These students have set their lives in motion by His Spirit. They have picked up His book and made it their First Book. What will you do?

"CHEAT SHEET" FOR FIRST BOOK CHALLENGE

This is not an endorsement of dishonesty but a helpful summary of the sections found in the four chapters of this book. Understanding the structure of each chapter will help you more effectively encounter God through Scripture.

We hope that as you accept the First Book Challenge, you will encounter God and His Word in a fresh way. Each chapter is made up of seven sections to help you experience His Word and the life He has for you:

Principle: This is the big idea phrased in a brief and memorable way — one thing you should be able to take away from the chapter and apply to your relationship with God. The principle is the hook on which the truth of the chapter hangs. The principle is meant to be memorable, understandable, and doable.

Passage: This is the passage of Scripture referenced throughout the chapter. Often Bible studies are filled with multiple references from different books of the Bible that require the reader to skip from book to book looking at the verses without much chance to absorb the content. Each chapter will explain the truth behind one passage with the intention of helping you encounter God and His Word. Make sure you have a Bible and pen with you while reading *First Book Challenge*. Visit www.firstbookchallenge.org for Bible resources and journals.

Unpacking the Passage: This section provides a list of questions that will help you internalize the Scripture and gain a sense of the message behind each passage. These questions are designed to get you to think about the text at a deeper level. Exhaustive responses are not required, just an opportunity to allow God's Word to stir your senses.

Off the Page: Reading Scripture can sometimes be challenging, especially in a culture of texting and tweeting. We all learn differently. Some think in facts and figures, while others think in pictures. This section provides new and buoyant ways to encounter Scripture and make it a part of your heart, mind, and soul.

Personal Download: Reading or hearing Scripture can be difficult when you don't see how it applies to your life. Studying the Bible involves more than just gathering information. It is through the steady act of applying Scripture that the reader reaches a deeper level of understanding. This section will lead you to take the passage and see how it applies to your personal environment, your circumstances, and the current choices you may be facing. In this section, you will view Scripture through the lenses of your life.

Live the Word: This section highlights students who have lived out the principles of Scripture by choosing to make God's Book their First Book. These are true stories of students who have faced struggles and challenges and have seen God do incredible things in their lives. These are encouraging stories, demonstrating how God and His Word cause amazing things to happen.

Heart Challenge: After each student's story, you will be challenged to respond directly and honestly to a few questions. These questions will allow you to reflect on how God is speaking and moving in your life. This section prods you to answer the question "What are you going to do about it?" Parts of these Bible studies may help you recognize that you are the answer to someone else's need. Your answer to God will determine the way in which you will respond to the First Book Challenge.

INTRODUCTION

What we need today is more of God's presence, but, sadly, God's Spirit seems to be lost somewhere in our current culture. Many students understand the need for God's presence in their lives but don't know what to do about it. You might be aware of the tension between your mind and heart. Your experience is based on what you understand, but often your reading is dry. Your heart is filled with emotions that don't lead in any particular direction. Faith seems to be experienced in two separate places, completely isolated from each other. In our thoughts, God is abstract. Much of our reading is about getting our ideas right, as though defining biblical beliefs might relieve the tension between our faith and actions. But the problem still remains that we are not stirred by what we know. There has been no outbreak of truth in our faith or actions. We have fallen into a pattern because our heads and hearts are separated. The pattern takes on a predictable form. We experience excitement about reading the Bible and knowing God, we find it challenging, we become disappointed with God and ourselves, and we get discouraged and tired. This is what life looks like when we try to live it ourselves.

This is why we need the Holy Spirit. It is the Holy Spirit's job to fill the space between head and heart. There is nothing more important than knowing the Holy Spirit. To miss out on the Spirit is to miss out on living Christianity. It is possible to keep *doing* Christian things yet not be living the Christian life because we have overlooked the Holy Spirit. It is the Holy Spirit who makes faith and the Word of God dynamic and active. The single most important component of Christianity is the Holy Spirit, who reveals all that God has for us. Our challenge is to experience life in the Spirit. Without the Holy Spirit, our own best efforts at doing the right thing prove that *good enough* is *not enough*. In this book, you will come face-to-face with the fact that you never stop needing the Spirit. Every Christian is indwelled by the Holy Spirit, but few experience all the works of the Spirit. The Spirit's work is highly practical. It produces ability, talent, and understanding about the heart of God and provides courage to do things you could not ordinarily do. In these extreme days of our lives, now more than ever, we need a work from the Holy Spirit.

The goal of the First Book Challenge is to help you make Scripture a priority in your life. This book focuses specifically on what the Bible has to say about the work of the Holy Spirit. In these four sessions, you will discover that your experience with God and all the choices you make that honor Him happened as a result of the boosting power of the Holy Spirit.

CHAPTER 1

JOIN IN

PRINCIPLE:
GOD WORKS FROM THE INSIDE OUT.

Extreme sports are stunts performed by people who will do anything to get a date. There are a wide variety of these types of activities, including BASE jumping from bridges and skyscrapers, downhill rollerblading, and riding BMX bicycles on a half-pipe. I define extreme sports as "psychotic behaviors of suicidal people who want to end their lives but don't want the pesky side effects of terminus abruptus." Why would anyone risk life and limb only to be slammed to the ground by wicked immovable obstacles? (But that's enough about math class.)

Recently I shopped in a store that caters to these psychotic adrenaline junkies. The clothing was expensive, the equipment was expensive, and the advertised venues hosting the events were expensive. The food was a wide selection of brightly wrapped multi-flavored, sawdust-injected, soy protein bars that could survive the Apocalypse and still be eaten, and they were expensive. If I ever actually participated in any of these activities, my wallet would take an extreme hit.

I remember when an extreme sport was cow tipping. Who can ever forget the thrill of waiting downwind for the cow to drop off to sleep and then creeping up on it, pushing it over, and running for dear life? Now, that's extreme!

Actually, surviving life is extreme enough. Try crossing the street in any major city or going to high school and hoping you make it through the day without someone squeezing off ten rounds from a nine-millimeter. How about driving down the California freeway, where both turn signals and handguns indicate, "I'm moving into your lane." Survive the night going on a blind date set up by your friends that forces you to spend an evening with a convicted felon.

Extreme sports are everywhere. Madison Avenue is no exception. I was watching TV and saw three young boys riding their skateboards through a park. They were playing an extreme version of follow the leader. They popped up over curbs, jumped over small dogs while spinning and flipping their boards, and then landed on a park bench, grinding it all the way to the end. I watched in amazement, because without this commercial, I would never have known that putting juice in a pouch gave it such an extreme flavor — I mean, flava. You know what I'm saying?

/ / / / / / / / / / /

We live in extreme days filled with the unexpected and we experience pressure from every side. We need something extra to make it through the extreme circumstances of our lives. Paul, the writer of Philippians, makes an obvious statement about the Christian life that often goes unnoticed: God is at work in us.

The word *in* indicates direction and location. This word is important to our study of the Holy Spirit because it describes the direction in which the Spirit moves and the location where the Spirit works. We encounter the work of the Spirit in our lives. Looking at the work of the Spirit as revealed in Scripture, we see the Spirit is at work in God's people.

The Holy Spirit is the driving force of insight about God. Scripture helps us appreciate the full scope of the work of the Holy Spirit. Though not originally written in the order we find them in today, the books of the Bible have been arranged into sections to give us a better understanding of the overall message of Scripture. Knowing how the major sections of the Bible are divided helps us understand to a greater degree the way the Holy Spirit is speaking.

The major sections of the Bible serve as folders that hold the individual books. Just like an app on a phone takes you to an experience, when you access one of the sixty-six books of the Bible, you experience God and His Spirit. The thirty-nine apps of the Old Testament are grouped into five folders: Law, History, Poetry, Major Prophets, and Minor Prophets. The twenty-seven apps of the New Testament are also placed into five folders: Gospels, History, Paul's Letters, General Letters, and Prophecy (see page 18).

The Bible is a record of the activity of God through history. This activity always involves the work of the Holy Spirit. The active work of the Spirit appears from Genesis to Revelation. In the beginning, God Himself is seen at work through His Spirit in creation as well as in historical and natural processes. In Scripture, nothing occurs by chance. Everything is the result of the active work of God through His Spirit. The Word of God makes it clear that the divine agent in the work of God and in the universe is the Spirit of the Lord.

The unifying element throughout the books of the Old and New Testament is the Holy Spirit. On every page of Scripture, the life, work, and words of the Spirit move in the lives of people. This matters to you because the Spirit who spoke these words to the people in Scripture is the same Spirit who is at work in you today. When you see how the Spirit is at work in the books of the Bible, you can know that the Spirit is also at work in you. The Spirit of God in you connects you with the Scripture — the Word of God comes to life. Being empowered by the Spirit does not just happen by staring at the text on the pages; it comes about by the interaction between the Word of God and the work of the Holy Spirit. Through the guidance of the Word of God and the Holy Spirit, the insight of the past meets the insight of the present. The Holy Spirit is alive and at work in you, bringing to life the always-

OLD TESTAMENT

The Law
- Genesis
- Exodus
- Leviticus
- Numbers
- Deuteronomy

History
- Joshua
- Judges
- Ruth
- 1 Samuel
- 2 Samuel
- 1 Kings
- 2 Kings
- 1 Chronicles
- 2 Chronicles
- Ezra
- Nehemiah
- Esther

Poetry
- Job
- Psalms
- Proverbs
- Ecclesiastes
- Song of Songs

Major
- Isaiah
- Jeremiah
- Lamentations
- Ezekiel
- Daniel

& Minor Prophets
- Hosea
- Joel
- Amos
- Obadiah
- Jonah
- Micah
- Nahum
- Habakkuk
- Zephaniah
- Haggai
- Zechariah
- Malachi

NEW TESTAMENT

Gospels
- Matthew
- Mark
- Luke
- John

History
- Acts

Paul's Letters
- Romans
- 1 Corinthians
- 2 Corinthians
- Galatians
- Ephesians
- Philippians
- Colossians
- 1 Thessalonians
- 2 Thessalonians
- 1 Timothy
- 2 Timothy
- Titus
- Philemon

General Letters
- Hebrews
- James
- 1 Peter
- 2 Peter
- 1 John
- 2 John
- 3 John
- Jude

Prophecy
- Revelation

relevant Word of the Lord. When the Word and the Spirit function together, it's the Holy Spirit who is at work in you.

Paul wrote from prison in Rome to the church at Philippi. This church was started during Paul's second missionary journey. The people of this church drew much of their faith and ability to serve from Paul's presence. Now that he was no longer with them, they grew tired and were not getting along with each other. Some had even pulled away from the faith. They had become discouraged because Paul wasn't there to motivate, encourage, inspire, and keep them progressing in the faith.

Paul reminded this church that their faith was not built on him or his charisma as their leader. They weren't dependent on him for their spiritual strength and growth. Paul had pastored and instructed them, but he could not live their lives of faith for them. The spiritual progress of the Philippians was not dependent on Paul or any external source. Paul explained to the Philippians that there was a driving force within them that enabled spiritual progress and raised every part of their lives to a new level. Paul reminded them that they didn't need him with them to grow spiritually. The Holy Spirit alone was doing a mighty work within them. Let's read how Paul communicated this thought to the Philippians.

PASSAGE:
PHILIPPIANS 2:12-13

My dear friends, as you have always obeyed — not only in my presence, but now much more in my absence — continue to work out your salvation with fear and trembling, for it is God who works in you to will and to act according to his good purpose.

Philippians 2:12-13 contains one of the most astonishing state-ments in Scripture and one of the most powerful summaries of the

Christian life: "It is God at work in you." Don't miss this! This verse really does mean *inside of you*. God is at work in the deepest parts of your life. He works on you from the inside out. There is no more radical idea than this truth that God takes the initiative to oversee spiritual progress in every part of your life.

"God is at work." What does this mean? The word *work* literally means "to energize." At the moment Christ becomes Lord of your life, you are given the boosting power of God's Spirit. The Spirit is the energizing work of God. Think of it: Every part of your life with God is made possible by the Spirit of God — all the thoughts you have that inspire you spiritually, all the desires you have to know Him more deeply, and all the choices you make that honor Him are produced by God's work in you. God, by the person and the work of the Spirit, helps empower your thoughts, emotions, and actions to create a life you didn't know you were capable of living. God is involved in the progress of your life from beginning to end. Spiritual life began with Him and He keeps it going. Nowhere in Scripture does it say that spiritual progress comes from effort. True faith cannot be self-generated or self-produced; it is the direct result of God at work. Are you aware of God's working in you? Becoming more aware that He is changing you from the inside out is proof that you are heading in the right direction and living more and more by the Spirit.

> God, by the person and the work of the Spirit, helps empower your thoughts, emotions, and actions to create a life you didn't know you were capable of living.

The best way to experience change from the inside out is to allow the Spirit to bring the Word of God to life as you involve yourself in it. Philippians 2:13 awakens us to the fact that God is at work in us and points out the truth that there is more to God than we are experiencing. The Holy Spirit is the person and the force that makes it possible for the Christian to experience God in his or her life. To most of us, the Holy Spirit seems mysterious. We find it difficult to convert Him into human form. Biblical symbols that represent the Holy Spirit in

Scripture — oil, fire, wind, dove — don't help us see the Holy Spirit as a real, personal part of the Trinity. We can get to know the Holy Spirit and experience His love within our lives. We can experience a greater level of relationship with Christ through His Spirit, even while living in a culture that elevates sinful facades over a real relationship with Christ.

This inside work is not a hope or wish but an actual work of God's Spirit. To understand this, we must know more about who the Spirit is. Jesus loves the Holy Spirit and He personally promised that the Spirit is our Helper, Counselor, and Friend. He is just as divine, just as strong, just as loving, and just as able to help us as God the Father and God the Son. He's always with us. This is one of the most powerful thoughts of the New Testament. The Holy Spirit is the cure for loneliness, broken hearts, fear, and danger. When it comes to our lives, the Holy Spirit knows what should be done and what should be said. If we join His work, we'll experience the help of God.

> The best way to experience change from the inside out is to allow the Spirit to bring the Word of God to life as you involve yourself in it.

There are definite outcomes of the Spirit working in you. In this session, we will unpack five of them.

1. The Holy Spirit changes the spiritual climate of our lives. Your relationship with the Holy Spirit is like a thermostat. Picture the thermostat in your spiritual life being controlled by the Holy Spirit. He will adjust your spiritual temperature up or down based on your request. When you allow Him to take control, your spiritual climate will reflect the temperature based on God's will for your life. Having the Holy Spirit take control may sound spooky. The way the Spirit gains control in our lives is not by overpowering us but by first working in the secret areas that we have been hiding — such as our faults and failures — and bringing them out in the open. Having the struggles of life exposed by God is a freeing process. When the darkest areas of our lives are revealed, the Holy Spirit shows us we have been loved, forgiven, and freed to live our lives out in the open. We live life in a new spiritual climate.

2. As the Holy Spirit continues to work in our lives, an authentic expression before God is produced. Authentic worship led by the Holy Spirit is one that demonstrates a commitment to God. Authentic worship requires true commitment, a complete change of life, and a willingness to follow the Holy Spirit as He directs. Worship is hard work for people who try time and again to cultivate a response that is not real. This empty effort comes from a faulty picture of God we carry in our minds. God is seen as irritated, demanding, and disappointed. The work of the Holy Spirit is to give us a new picture, a true view of Jesus. As the Spirit brings us out of our old distorted images of Jesus and shows us who He really is, we find a new passion for God's presence. As the Holy Spirit makes Jesus real to us, authentic worship is triggered, both in our personal lives and in worship with our community of faith.

> The way the Spirit gains control in our lives is not by overpowering us but by first working in the secret areas that we have been hiding — such as our faults and failures — and bringing them out in the open.

3. The Holy Spirit works in our lives to bring about self-control in our personal choices as well as in our social behavior. Self-control is the result of the influence of the Holy Spirit in our whole lives, realizing it produces outward changes in our moral choices. To see the work of the Spirit in your life, look at the choices you are making emotionally and physically. Do they show evidence that God is at work in you?

Our lives are far from perfect. The lies of the Enemy have affected our emotional makeup. For our response to change, we must first possess a level of honesty about the way we're living. It's at the point of honesty that the Holy Spirit enters and brings a new way of experiencing and expressing the work of God. It's not that we become robots. Rather, the Holy Spirit helps us leave behind destructive behavior and brings godly emotions to life. The Holy Spirit fans into flame the full spectrum of healthy choices and right responses that honor God in our relationships.

4. As the Spirit works in us, loving others is easier. We need the Spirit to do the changing on the inside of our lives. We are called to follow Jesus in every way. The core of this is the call to love. To love others as Jesus did is what Christianity is all about. We are called to love God, each other, and our enemies. Even though we know we should love others, we often don't. It's the work of the Spirit that changes our hearts to reflect the love we are called to give and show.

> It's the work of the Spirit that changes our hearts to reflect the love we are called to give and show.

5. The Spirit produces real Christians through us. This is made possible by the Spirit empowering people to live with extraordinary courage – the spirit of fearlessness – for the sake of Christ. The Bible is filled with people who spoke boldly about the risen Jesus. They were empowered with zeal to tell others about Christ. The mission of the Christian's life has always been to bring others to Christ by reaching out to those who have not heard, to those who have heard but walked away, and to those who have ignored Christ.

> God desires to be at work in you. His work is the source of energy for a vibrant life of faith.

Philippians 2 makes it clear that God desires to be at work in you. His work is the source of energy for a vibrant life of faith. He is always at work. It's a work that never stops. Through His Spirit, He is radically changing your life from the inside out. Instead of being distracted by outside influences, why not join in?

⍰ UNPACKING THE PASSAGE

1. What types of individuals is Paul writing this letter to? Describe the recipients of this letter.

2. What does the phrase "God is at work" mean?

3. When God works in our lives, where does He go to work first? How does He do it?

4. Why does God work in our lives through His Spirit? As a result of His work, how should we conduct our lives?

OFF THE PAGE

Prayer is vitally important when reading Scripture. When studying the Bible, there are three specific times you should pray: as you start reading, during your reading, and after you read. As you start reading, it is helpful to pray something like, "Dear God, I cannot understand any of this unless You explain it to me. I'm here, willing to hear from You and do whatever Your Word says." As you move further into your reading, it's helpful to stop and pray, "God, give me insight that will lead me to discovering more about You." As you bring your reading to a close, pray Philippians 2:12-13 in the first person back to God aloud. As you read these verses, insert your name. When you hear yourself praying the promises of God, you will be amazed what happens.

When was the last time you stopped and realized that God is at work within you? Stop right now and ask Him to reveal where He is at work in you. When Jesus becomes the leader of your life, you receive the gift of the Holy Spirit. God sends us a Holy Helper. Jesus refers to Him as the Counselor. Often we miss out on His guidance and friendship because we aren't looking for Him.

PERSONAL DOWNLOAD

Reread Philippians 2:12-13, the chapter's passage. The following questions and suggestion for memorization will help you apply the principle of this chapter to your life and strengthen you in your journey toward being more like Christ.

1. Describe why we typically want God to do something on the outside of our lives before we allow Him to transform the inside of our lives.

2. Why do we struggle with allowing the Spirit to control the spiritual climate of our lives?

3. Describe a time in your life when you were engaged in authentic worship. What does authentic worship look like outside of a church building?

4. Why do we struggle with submission? What are the benefits of having the ability to control our internal emotions? Why is it imperative that we are totally controlled by the Spirit?

5. Commit Philippians 2:13 to memory. This verse will remind you that God is the sole source of power in your life. He desires to guide and direct you to follow His good purposes for you. His Word is packed with power.

//

💬 LIVE THE WORD

Robert wanted to share about his relationship with Christ on a weekly basis at the mission house in downtown Dallas. It was on one of these trips that Robert came across a young woman with two small children and began to share with the woman what it means to have a true relationship with Christ. As he began to speak to her, he could see in her eyes that something was wrong. Before he knew it, she raised her hand and smacked him across the face!

That's right. A huge "Get out of my life" smack hit him in the face. Robert described the slap as surreal and matrix-like, moving slowly through the air and then pressing against his face with an incredible amount of pain. This young lady spoke to Robert as he stood speechless. Her statement was simply this: "You guys tell me how to get saved, but you do nothing to help me." He could immediately see there was a lot more going on here and knew he would be able to continue to minister to this woman only by relying on the strength of the Holy Spirit.

Robert had a decision to make. It was while making this decision that he remembered a passage he had committed to memory — Philippians 2:12-13. At this crucial moment, he recalled the truth found in that passage: It is God's presence working in us and through our lives that accomplishes His purpose. The passage not only gave Robert the answer to his situation but also reminded him of God's love for people and the heart Christians need to have to share that love with others.

What transpired was remarkable. Over the course of a month, Robert continued to build a relationship with this young woman and her two small children. He wasn't worried about getting everything fixed in order for the family to enter into a relationship with Christ. Nor was it about doing a bunch of things somebody had listed on a task sheet. He shared with her that everyone is equal at the feet of Jesus. She could come to Christ with all of her problems and struggles and invite Him into her life. Robert honestly shared that although her issues may not disappear, she would never have to worry about moving through life alone. She would now have the presence of the Holy Spirit in her life. Not only would the Spirit be there to help and guide her, He would also be there to bring her great comfort and security every day of her life. She gave her heart to the Lord, and Robert was also able to share with the woman's sister what it meant to have a relationship with Christ. As time progressed, he was able to help find them a home and jobs. Most important, he established hope for this young mother and her family outside the walls of the Dallas mission.

Go to www.firstbookchallenge.org to tell us your story about how God and His Word have made a difference in your life, friends, family, school, and church.

///

 HEART CHALLENGE

We need the work of the Spirit to release the love of God in our lives. The desire and ability to love others flow from the Spirit. As a result of the Spirit's working in us, we move beyond superficial love to genuine care of and investment in others.

1. When you consider Robert's situation, how would you have reacted to a smack in the face? Would you say that most Christians share their faith out of obligation, or are they led to do so out of the passion they have for Christ? Please explain your answer.

2. How has the Holy Spirit's internal guidance in your life transformed your spiritual climate from simply *doing* a bunch of religious tasks to *becoming* Christlike?

3. Describe a time in your life when you allowed emotional control to impact you spiritually. Contrast it with a time when you were able to worship authentically as an expression of your relationship with God.

WRITE COOL STUFF HERE

WRITE COOL STUFF HERE

WRITE COOL STUFF HERE

CHAPTER 2

LIFE BOOST

PRINCIPLE:
THE HOLY SPIRIT LEADS US
TO THE LIFE OF JESUS.

Growing up, whenever I heard about the Holy Spirit or Holy "Ghost," it kind of freaked me out. I would hear about God the Father, and I could handle that. I understood God the Son. My great-aunt Voncille had a picture of Jesus' face on the mantle along with the rest of our school pictures. (Obviously, Jesus' mom didn't make Him get a haircut for picture day like my mom did.) But God the Holy Spirit seemed like some sort of weird cousin Eddie who was awkward to talk about.

Whenever I would hear about a church that was deep into the Holy Spirit, I thought they were spooky. I assumed the Holy Spirit hung out only with ladies with hair buns who took fashion cues from Little House on the Prairie *and guys on TV who tried to get me to buy a medicine dropper full of water from the River Jordan. I didn't know either of these types of people personally, so I just figured I would be fine with God and Jesus. I would leave the Holy Spirit to the people with their tambourines and strange languages. I just didn't understand what all the fuss was about.*

///////////

Many Christians have had the same problem understanding the role of the Holy Spirit. This has led some people to either just ignore the Spirit altogether or develop arbitrary expectations of Him. Many people treat the Holy Spirit like some sort of heavenly McDonald's. They drive up, wait for Him to speak through the intercom, but never understand what He says, so they just start placing their order anyway: "Um, yeah, I'd like a new job with a supersize salary, hold the cold I've been fighting, and a girlfriend – but don't supersize her, please." Then, when they pull away from the window, they are bitter because they didn't get what they ordered. But this isn't the purpose of the Holy Spirit. He isn't a servant to us. He is God's presence working in us to help us grow to our full potential in Christ. Christ promised that the Holy Spirit would be with us. God didn't leave us here to figure things out on our own and do the best we could to live full lives. He sent His Spirit to guide us throughout our walk with Him.

> God didn't leave us here to figure things out on our own and do the best we could to live full lives. He sent His Spirit to guide us throughout our walk with Him.

The Holy Spirit is usually treated as a lost member of a close family. It's as if He is a long-lost cousin who was adopted into the family of God – you know, the one who attends the family reunion at Christmas but you never really know who he belongs to. The problem is that we view the Spirit as some type of spiritual mist floating through the heavenly realms instead of the personal presence of God that dwells within us and desires to work with and through us.

Those who seek to experience more of the Holy Spirit will never be disappointed. There is nothing to fear by encountering Him. Simply ask, "Is what we know of the Holy Spirit biblical? Do our beliefs have their foundation in Scripture?" Scripture is God's message to us. The Bible is the textbook on the things of God, including the Holy Spirit. We must call on the wisdom found in God's Word when we encounter His Spirit.

The Bible teaches us about the work of the Holy Spirit. Though the Holy Spirit is invisible, He's very real. The Holy Spirit is a person and is referred to as "Him." He's shown continually in Scripture acting in personal ways. The Bible says that He can be hurt, lied to, received, grieved, and known. The Spirit gives life. He's with us now. Scripture speaks of Jesus being in heaven and the Spirit being at work on earth. It's through the work of the Spirit that we know the Father and the Son. Without the Spirit, we can't know spiritual things. The Spirit has come from heaven and only He knows how to make the things of Jesus real in us. We are dependent upon the Spirit for everything in our Christian lives. We can't experience the full life of faith without the work of the Spirit. The work of the Spirit leads to the life of Jesus. This session's focus is on just that.

The apostle Paul had experienced this principle firsthand. Paul was the most unlikely guy to become a devoted follower of Christ. He had spent most of his life as a religious bully. Often he would tell the story of his conversion by sharing how Christ had been revealed in him. His life had been revolutionized by the Holy Spirit. It's no surprise that in his writing, Paul placed great emphasis on the work of the Spirit.

> The Holy Spirit isn't a servant to us. He is God's presence working in us to help us grow to our full potential in Christ.

Paul wrote this letter to the church at Ephesus not to impress them with his intellect or to debate doctrine but to help them find a new power for living and encourage them to grow in their faith. The church at Ephesus was strong in the basics of Christian faith, but they hadn't grown beyond that point since their conversion. Life continued to move forward, but the faith of the Ephesians remained stuck in the past. They needed a deeper experience of who Christ was. This would involve cooperating with the Holy Spirit to experience Jesus in a vivid, dynamic, and transforming way. It would take the Holy Spirit to make Jesus real to them. The passion of the Holy Spirit is to point us to Jesus.

⬤ PASSAGE:
EPHESIANS 3:16-19

I pray that out of his glorious riches he may strengthen you with power through his Spirit in your inner being, so that Christ may dwell in your hearts through faith. And I pray that you, being rooted and established in love, may have power, together with all the saints, to grasp how wide and long and high and deep is the love of Christ, and to know this love that surpasses knowledge — that you may be filled to the measure of all the fullness of God.

Experiencing the life of Jesus is not just an idea. Ephesians 3:16-19 describes our need for Jesus, along with the depth and dimension of the work of the Holy Spirit as the Spirit applies the life of Christ to us. "He would grant you . . . to be strengthened with power through His Spirit in the inner man" (verse 16, NASB). The phrase "to be strengthened" challenges us to never be satisfied with where we are in our relationship with Jesus but, by the Spirit, to be constantly growing and deepening our love for and commitment to Jesus. This will make us aware of the need to be stronger spiritually.

The Holy Spirit strengthens **our spiritual intelligence.** We develop a deeper understanding of the great truth of God's *words.* All of us have experienced our thoughts wandering while we try to read Scripture. Sometimes it is difficult to concentrate, but as the inner man is strengthened in us, the ability to stay engaged with Scripture becomes greater. The work of the Holy Spirit also strengthens **our thought life.** When we have thoughts that cause us to doubt God, strengthening the inner man produces truth-filled thinking. **Our hearts** need to be strengthened in the same way our spiritual lives strengthen our minds. Discouragement can hit us hard and flood our hearts with many negative emotions. Without the strengthening of the inner man, our lives can be derailed by negativity. **Our will** needs to be stronger. Many times we get caught in a cycle of making promises to God and then breaking them. This is a challenge in our relationship with Christ because we make promises we don't intend to keep. Strengthening **our inner man** helps us make better choices and keep the promises we make to God.

Now let's look at some phrases from these verses in Ephesians 3 that show why the work of the Holy Spirit is so important in our lives.

Verse 16 drives home the point of how we are made stronger by using the phrase "through His Spirit." It is the special function of the Holy Spirit to strengthen our inner man — not just to make us better people but to make more room for the Life of Jesus.

Verse 17 opens with the words "so that Christ may dwell in your hearts." The word *dwell* means "to settle down in, to live in a certain place." Think of the difference between visiting your friends' homes and being at home. In your friends' homes, you are a guest; in your home, you create the atmosphere because you belong there. In the same way, Jesus is not to be simply a guest in our lives. It is the presence of the Spirit that creates the atmosphere for Jesus in our lives.

He makes Himself at home. The work of the Holy Spirit is not in any way a substitute for Jesus, but rather it is the Spirit who makes Jesus obvious and applies the Life of Jesus into all the details of our lives. The result is that we become a dwelling place for the Life of Christ.

As we understood in the last session, God knew that if we were to enter into a saving relationship with Him, He would have to not only be revealed *to* us but also *in* us. God did not stop by sending His Son to dwell *among* us; He also sent His Spirit to reside *within* us. Not only does God speak *to* us but He also lives out His truth *in* His Son and gives us access to His life *through* His Spirit. The Holy Spirit applies the Life of Jesus and guides believers into the truth by pointing them to Jesus. Here are four practical ways the Holy Spirit works in our lives.

> The work of the Holy Spirit is not in any way a substitute for Jesus, but rather it is the Spirit who makes Jesus obvious and applies the Life of Jesus into all the details of our lives. The result is that we become a dwelling place for the Life of Christ.

1. The Spirit *teaches* us God's truth. Why is it that so many believers experience such little success in their spiritual growth? Often they try to grow spiritually without the help of the Spirit. The truth of God can be understood only when the Spirit teaches us. The teaching of the Spirit is different from accessing other types of information. It's done in a practical way that inspires the way we live. It will never make us arrogant but increases a sense of humility. It produces a deeper hunger for spiritual things and always brings about a positive change in our lives.

Because of the personal salvation we receive in Christ, we become untouchable. The presence of the Holy Spirit provides total freedom. We are no longer trapped by hypocrisy, pretending to be spiritual. The Holy Spirit brings freedom. He pulls us from a life of falsehood and gives us the freedom to be who God originally created us to be. This freeing work of the Holy Spirit impacts our beliefs, talents, and choices. Because of the work of the Spirit, we have a whole new reference point by which to live. The Spirit does not take us on some tangent but always points us to the presence of Jesus. We have nothing to fear in encountering the Holy Spirit.

2. The Spirit *guides* us through our daily lives. There's a connection between guidance and direction. This work of guidance is particularly the work of the Spirit. The Spirit keeps us moving in the right direction by keeping the Word of God stirred up in our mind, dealing with our conscience, and adjusting our desires and conduct. The Holy Spirit will never direct us to act contrary to the ways and the Word of God. The believer doesn't ever have to walk in the dark. He's free to ask and receive direction from the Spirit through the various means He uses. Our challenge is to ensure that we don't limit the Spirit's movement in our lives by saying such things as "He isn't supposed to do it that way" or "He should do it this way." The Holy Spirit is God. He is a part of the Trinity and will guide us along this journey according to His will, not ours.

The guidance of the Spirit is a gentle and consistent influence that moves us toward God's truth by speaking, teaching, and reminding us of

Jesus' life and ministry. The Holy Spirit teaches God's wisdom and applies it to our lives. As the Spirit guides us in the ways of Christ, we learn how to handle the challenging circumstances that come our way.

3. The Spirit *assures* us that we have nothing to fear because we belong to Him. The Spirit is also the One who assures the Christian that he or she belongs to God. The believer shares in the life of the Father as a member of His family. He also becomes an heir of God. Assurance of inheritance is the work of the Spirit in the heart of each Christian.

Doubting our salvation is common. Many Christians struggle with the assurance of their salvation. Thankfully, we don't have to go through life being unsure. Confidence in our connection to Jesus is most important because it affects our eternal destiny and spiritual growth.

How can we know that we have genuinely believed in Jesus? We cannot rely on our feelings because they can mislead us. Simply knowing the facts of the gospel doesn't mean we believe in Jesus. A transformation must take place that can be prompted only by the Holy Spirit. Destructive thoughts and behavior are replaced with choices shaped by the work

> Simply knowing the facts of the gospel doesn't mean we believe in Jesus. A transformation must take place that can be prompted only by the Holy Spirit.

of God that result in a genuine love for others and an increasing affection for the interests of God. The Holy Spirit gives us full confidence that Jesus is the substance of our faith and a certainty that we are eternally kept by the Lord. The evidence that we belong to Him is our thinking highly of God and depending upon Him to live faithfully. Also, there is a living love for God accompanied by a willingness to do what He asks. Through the work of the Holy Spirit, we are given assurance knowing that we belong to God.

4. The Spirit continually *prays* for us. Although we may not fully understand the ramifications of the Spirit's prayer, the fact that He does pray is perfectly clear. We need the prayers of the Spirit because of our weakness. He helps us in our weakness, particularly in the areas of knowing how to pray and what to pray for at any given moment. We often do not know our needs, only our wants, and a believer should never be reluctant to express his or her wants as long as they are according to the will of God. The Spirit knows our needs and the needs of others. He will pray according to the will of God. While we wait for our full redemption, we need guidance in the specifics of prayer.

Talking to God can be difficult. Often we don't know what to say. When we do speak, our words sound weak and hollow. When life becomes chaotic, prayer is especially necessary and sometimes difficult. The solution to praying effectively is to realize the Holy Spirit joins us when we pray. He prays for us when our words feel frail and we don't know what to say. The Spirit searches our hearts, knows the mind of God, and prays the will of God for us. The Holy Spirit prays with us in real time. He prays *with* us and *for* us. The Spirit absorbs our words and teaches us what it means to pray in the Spirit. We have everything to gain and nothing to fear from the work of the Spirit because the Holy Spirit always points us to Jesus. It's easy to see just how much we need both the presence and the work of the Holy Spirit. There is nothing to fear in the empowering work of the Spirit.

> We have everything to gain and nothing to fear from the work of the Spirit because the Holy Spirit always points us to Jesus.

Before finishing the rest of this chapter, take a moment to pray by saying, "Holy Spirit, You are welcome in my life."

⊙ UNPACKING THE PASSAGE

1. In these verses, Paul prays for the Ephesians. Of all the things he could have prayed for, why did he pray that they would experience the work of the Holy Spirit?

2. How is the work of the Holy Spirit connected to experiencing Jesus?

3. Have you experienced the work of the Holy Spirit reminding you of what Jesus taught you in the past? Describe the experience.

4. How does the Spirit's work of pointing and leading you to Jesus help you be more open to the leadership of the Spirit?

👓 OFF THE PAGE

If you approach Scripture by saying, "I've already read this passage before," you will be robbed of discovering new insight from God's Word. Assuming we already know what Scripture says because we've heard it, read it, or know the story line limits what the Spirit can reveal as we read it. The Bible continues to speak to people. It has lasted for thousands of years and withstood the test of time.

Don't just read a verse and then move on to the next one; instead, read a verse over and over again. Read Ephesians 3:16-19 four times a day for the next four days. Make notes of the different things you discover each time you read it. Staying in a passage for an extended amount of time and reading it at different times during the day and in different places will help you discover new truths.

🔁 PERSONAL DOWNLOAD

Reread Ephesians 3:16-19, the chapter's passage. The following questions and suggestion for memorization will help you apply the principle of this chapter to your life and strengthen you in your journey toward being more like Christ.

1. Read these verses and then rewrite them as a prayer. Pray the prayer, welcoming the work of the Holy Spirit into your life. Take your time.

2. The inner man of verse 16 strengthens our thoughts, feelings, and actions. In what specific areas do you need to become stronger?

3. Is Christ a temporary guest or permanent resident in your heart?

4. Why is the Holy Spirit necessary in order for us to have a more vivid experience with Jesus?

5. Commit Ephesians 3:16 to memory. This verse will remind you that you are not alone. God provided His Holy Spirit to live in you and remind you of the person of Jesus Christ. The Holy Spirit makes it possible for you to understand God's Word.

//

💬 LIVE THE WORD

Nicky was born into a troubled home. She attended church for the first time in her life on a Wednesday night. She wanted so desperately to experience the love, mercy, and grace of Jesus that was spoken about. These were new words for Nicky. The fact that someone loved and cared for her so much that He would give up His life were words that she had never heard.

It wasn't long after Nicky began attending that the Holy Spirit gave her a burning desire to have a relationship with Jesus. One Wednesday, her youth pastor began teaching from Ephesians 3:14-19. It was while he spoke that the Holy Spirit began to minister and speak to her. Nicky began to understand who God was and what He was all about. The love and relationship revealed through Scripture was something she desired. She made a decision to get away from the junk and pain of her life and turn to Christ. The Holy Spirit brought the love of Jesus to live in her heart. She embraced His love and mercy and took all of her problems and placed them at His feet.

Go to www.firstbookchallenge.org to tell us your story about how God and His Word have made a difference in your life, friends, family, school, and church.

//

🔑 HEART CHALLENGE

Commitment is a word that's used flippantly, especially when dealing with relationships. But for some, the word *commitment* is a word used to describe their relationship with Christ. When it comes to your commitment to Christ, be a faithful believer. Give Him everything you have so your life can be used for His glory.

1. How does the Holy Spirit make knowing and committing to Jesus easier? Can you think of a time in your life when you were able to know Jesus better because of the work of the Spirit in your life? Please explain.

2. Is God calling you to do something unusual with your life? Is there an area in your life that you're holding on to? What will it take for you to turn it over to the Lord?

3. Take a moment right now to ask God to reveal the parts of your life you refuse to give to Him. Take time to reflect on these areas. Then make a conscious decision to be the person He created you to be and live the life He intends for you to live!

WRITE COOL STUFF HERE

WRITE **COOL** STUFF HERE

CHAPTER 3

WALK ON

PRINCIPLE:
WHEN THE BEST AND WORST OF US COLLIDE, WE MUST CHOOSE SIDES.

Okay, I'll admit it. I tend to be a bit of a whiner. And after eight straight weeks on the road in airport after airport, there are times when I will spend an entire cross-country flight wallowing in self-pity (especially if they are out of honey-roasted peanuts and I have to settle for the plain ones!). I know you find this hard to believe. I know what you are thinking: You? Whiny?

Well, catch me at 11 p.m. in a window seat next to the guy whose laptop screen is lit up like NASA's command central and you may go back to your youth group with a few shocking stories to tell about that speaker guy. The truth is, I get irritable. But I don't want to be the grumpy passenger. I don't want to get home and growl at my family. In an effort to talk myself down and remind myself that my life could be much worse, I close my eyes, take a deep breath, and ask myself:

- *Does the word* penitentiary *appear anywhere in your mailing address?*
- *Did you contract a rare disease from a bug bite in the jungle and lose your ability to taste everything but pickles?*
- *Did your mom post pictures of your unfortunate "fifth-grade morbidly obese" phase on Facebook?*

- *Did you close on a house on Beach Boulevard in Biloxi the Thursday before Hurricane Katrina?*
- *Did God call you to spend your life wandering around the desert wearing sackcloth and eating locusts?*

If I can't answer yes to any of these questions, I calmly suggest to myself that I chill out and remember that my small little travel nightmares are minor inconveniences. I really do lead a blessed life. Now when guy-who-smells-like-beef-and-cheese stops in front of me in the airplane and slowly folds his coat into the overhead compartment like he is a member of the color guard flag folding team at a military funeral, I manage to refrain from looking to the heavens and screaming, "Why, God? Whyyyyy?"

I can't take credit for my improvement in the crabbiness area. Several years ago, after one particularly trying airport adventure (that I will not bore you with except to say it involved a screaming baby and her sleeping mother), I spent two hours of my life stomping around my hotel room stewing over how much I hate to travel. Finally, I got a genius idea: Why not practice what I preach and ask the Holy Spirit to help me with my attitude? I knew that my crankiness was not beneficial to anyone, least of all myself. I asked God to change me so that I would be able to obey Him.

/ / / / / / / / / / /

Many individuals feel like there is always a battle in life between the negative and the positive, between what they *want* to do and what they *should* do. The desires of natural emotions mixed with a toxic spirit are always trying to get the best of us. It seems like there is no way to deal with these evil impulses. We hunger for the things that we know are bad for us. It's in the midst of this battle that the Holy Spirit enters.

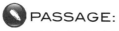 PASSAGE:
GALATIANS 5:16-17,25

Live by the Spirit, and you will not gratify the desires of the sinful nature. For the sinful nature desires what is contrary to the Spirit, and the Spirit what is contrary to the sinful nature. They are in conflict with each other, so that you do not do what you want. . . .

Since we live by the Spirit, let us keep in step with the Spirit.

The spiritual knockout punch of this battle is the focus of the book of Galatians. It is important to understand how this conflict between two natures was experienced in the Galatian church. The first converts to Christianity were Jewish. They had a religious background of following all the Old Testament rules and rituals. For the sake of this study, we will call them *law lovers*. Paul had begun to take the gospel into heavily populated areas so that as many people as possible could hear the message of Jesus. Many new converts resulted and the Galatian church was formed. We will refer to these new converts as *Lord lovers*.

> We hunger for the things that we know are bad for us. It's in the midst of this battle that the Holy Spirit enters.

The doors of this new church were open to everyone, religious and nonreligious. Everybody could access God through Jesus by faith alone. This sudden growth was too much for the *law lovers*. Their real thoughts and attitudes began to surface, and they could not hide their religious pride. The tension began to heighten. The *law lovers* did not want to deny anyone access to Christ, but they also believed there had to be more to following Jesus than just an act of faith. The *law lovers* wanted the *Lord lovers* to follow all the laws of Moses. The *law lovers* wanted to add to the simple message of the gospel. The *law lovers* and the *Lord lovers* began to collide in a battle between rules and relationship, laws and love.

The conflict within the church increased. In response, Paul wrote his letter to the Galatians. Paul redefined what it meant for both groups to follow Christ. He pointed them in the direction that would bring about a radical shift in faith.

The message in Galatians is clear: The heart of Christianity is Jesus. This defines our motivation and the choices we make to live a life of faith. On a personal level, we all have a *law lover* and a *Lord lover* inside of us. Every Christian fights this battle. When the best of us collides with the worst of us, we must choose to live by the Spirit. We are to live by the Spirit.

The word *live* in verse 16 is literally the word *walk*. The picture here is that the spiritual life is a process of walking. This is where the idea of the spiritual life being a journey comes from — the idea that commitment to Christ isn't a destination but the beginning of a pilgrimage from where we are today to where God wants to take us. This walk is an uphill one. There's conflict between the leftovers of our old way of life — called the desires of the flesh — and where the Holy Spirit is leading us. It's a conflict between what we want to do and where He wants us to go. The only way to make progress in this walk is to keep in step with the Spirit, just like a marching band keeps in step with its bandleader.

> Commitment to Christ isn't a destination but the beginning of a pilgrimage from where we are today to where God wants to take us.

This image of walking presents the Holy Spirit as being kind of like a coach. Coaching is a hands-on, relational process of helping a person become successful. The coach offers encouragement, resources, and help for the athlete to live up to his or her athletic potential. Similarly, the Holy Spirit offers us hands-on encouragement, resources, and help as we walk up this sometimes-steep hill of spiritual growth and maturity. Like a good coach, the Holy Spirit won't walk for us, but He walks side by side with us, inviting us to keep in step with His promptings, follow His direction, and rely on His encouragement and strengthening.

Because the Holy Spirit empowers our lives, we are free to move forward spiritually. Like a hiker climbing up a steep trail, we often feel like quitting or going back down the hill. We easily get distracted or lost. As our coach, the Holy Spirit helps us stay on the trail. He gives us water when we're thirsty, rest when we're tired, a kick in the pants when we grow lazy, and words of encouragement when we feel like quitting. The Bible calls this being filled with the Spirit.

It is vital to the life of every believer to be filled by the Spirit. Every person attempts to fill his or her life with something — friends, technology, love, fun, possessions — only to still feel empty. It's the will of God that every person would be filled with the Spirit.

Two words used in the New Testament in relation to the work of the Holy Spirit are *full* and *filled*. Understanding the difference between the two will help us experience the Holy Spirit and win the battle between our two natures. Being "full" of the Spirit is what happens at salvation. *Full* describes the kind of people we are and will always be in Christ. Being "filled" refers to being under the control, or empowerment, of the Spirit. For instance, consuming an energy drink *fills* you with levels of caffeine that can keep you awake for seventy-two hours. For that period of time, you are under the control of that substance. There is a momentary boost of energy. Every part of your life is influenced by that drink. But eventually it wears off. If you drink another can, you will be *filled* again. Likewise, we are to be *filled* with the Holy Spirit every day. That *filling* empowers us to face challenges, successfully take on tasks placed before us, and courageously serve the Lord. We tap into the resource of the Holy Spirit for strength. As we use the spiritual strength God provides, we must be *refilled*.

The spiritual life that follows Jesus Christ is not an easy stroll through the park, but it's a lifelong journey of transformation where we are changed into people who love God with our whole hearts and who love other people sacrificially. Sometimes the trail looks dangerous. Sometimes it looks outright impossible. We face challenges that threaten to overwhelm us. Sometimes we get lost. We defiantly sit down and refuse to go any further. Some people find the road too difficult. Some turn away. Some start back down the hill. No matter what we encounter along this lifelong trail, our Coach is with us, offering everything we need to take the next step. Are you stuck? Is your spiritual life any different today than it was a year ago? Are you discouraged? Feel like quitting or turning back? Where the Spirit of the Lord is, there is freedom to move forward.

Galatians makes it clear that there is a battle that goes on in our lives every day. It is not difficult to figure out. In fact, these verses summarize the battle by naming each side — the Spirit and the flesh — and showing us the choice we have to make in the battle. The inner work of the Spirit affects our moral lives. Galatians describes the war between the flesh and the Spirit. The flesh is the result of our fallen nature wanting to be the dominant force in our lives. This word *flesh* might need an explanation. It does not mean the skin that covers our bodies. *Flesh* is the Bible's word for the worst part of us. Leaving off the "h" in the word *flesh* and spelling it backward, you have the word *self*. *Flesh* is self-life. It's living selfishly.

> The spiritual life that follows Jesus Christ is not an easy stroll through the park, but it's a lifelong journey of transformation where we are changed into people who love God with our whole hearts and who love other people sacrificially.

So that we have an understanding of what the characteristic of selfishness looks like, Galatians 5:19-21 lists fifteen desires of the *flesh*. (Take a moment right now to reread these verses. See if you identify with any of these categories.) Likewise, the Spirit works to make the will of God the dominant force in our lives. These works of *self* can be overcome only by the work of the Spirit.

The evidence that the Spirit is winning the battle and that we are living in step with the presence of Jesus is seen in the visible evidence of the nine proofs — or fruit — of our lives. "The fruit of the Spirit is love, joy, peace, patience, kindness, goodness, faithfulness, gentleness and self-control. Against such things there is no law" (Galatians 5:22-23).

Our role in the battle between the flesh and the Spirit is to daily choose sides.

All of these proofs are the result of the Spirit making our relationship with Christ real in us. We don't work to produce this fruit; it is the result of the Spirit of God winning in our lives. Our role in the battle between the flesh and the Spirit is to daily choose sides.

(?) UNPACKING THE PASSAGE

1. According to these verses, what two forces are at war in our lives?

2. Do these verses give a command or offer a choice to be made? Why does this matter, and how does this affect our spiritual lives?

3. What do these verses say God's Spirit gives us the power to do?

4. What is the proof that the Spirit is defeating the flesh?

5. Why is it important that you have the Spirit in your life and allow Him to lead you in this journey?

OFF THE PAGE

God speaks to us through Scripture. Getting to know the Bible is like getting to know a person. You have to ask the right questions to get to know who He really is. The same is true for Scripture. You have to know the right questions. Take your Bible study to a new level. Ask the following questions of Galatians 5:16-17,25 or any passage you are studying.

- **What are the facts?** Are there positive and negative things about these verses? List what you observe in the verses no matter how insignificant the details may seem.
- **Why does it matter?** God had a reason for putting every verse in the Bible because He knew it would be important for our lives. In one sentence, state the point of these verses.
- **What are you going to do with it?** The Word of God is real and its words are true, but they are only words until you do something with them. What action are these verses asking of you — to live faithfully, to challenge an area of your life, to be courageous in a decision? What choice are these verses calling you to make?

PERSONAL DOWNLOAD

Reread Galatians 5:16-17,25, the chapter's passage. The following questions and suggestion for memorization will help you apply the principle of this chapter to your life and strengthen you in your journey toward being more like Christ.

1. How have you recently felt the tension between the powers of the flesh and the Spirit? Who was involved? What was the situation?

2. How do you feel when the flesh is winning?

3. How do you feel when the Spirit is winning?

4. Have you most recently seen evidence of the flesh or the Spirit winning the battles in your life? What do you need to do to allow God's Spirit to grow stronger in your life?

5. Commit Galatians 5:25 to memory. This verse will remind you that you are not alone. God provided His Holy Spirit to live in you and remind you of the person of Jesus Christ. The Holy Spirit makes it possible for you to understand God's Word.

//

💬 LIVE THE WORD

Christy was a young girl who had a great relationship with Christ. She decided to make a difference. She had the passion and conviction by the Spirit to do something, along with the God-given skill and ability to get it done. The struggle she faced was the same conflict many students face today. She had to confront this question: "Should I focus on myself to strengthen my own status among my peers, or should I use my influence to help those with no influence?" During a group devotion, she came across a passage from Galatians 5:16-17. The more she read, the clearer it became. Even though the flesh collides with the desires of the Spirit, Christy knew she had to choose the desire of the Spirit. It was the words of this passage that moved her to use her skill in softball and her leadership abilities to make a difference halfway across the world in India.

She decided to share her vision, love, and passion to see the babies in India rescued and given a chance to grow up to become believers and followers of Christ. Christy began to share her vision and, before long, had recruited enough volunteers and coaches to dedicate their time to see her vision come to life. Christy advertised a girls' softball camp that not only provided training but also gave those who attended the camp the opportunity to hear about the love of Christ. None of the registration fees collected was used to buy bats, softballs, or gloves. She didn't spend the money for a new dress or cell phone. All the money collected went toward saving baby girls in India. As a result of her two-day training camp, more than thirty-six babies on the other side of the world were saved, all because she said, "Enough is enough. I'm going to do something about it. I'm going to make a difference."

Go to www.firstbookchallenge.org to tell us your story about how God and His Word have made a difference in your life, friends, family, school, and church.

///

 HEART CHALLENGE

Are you willing to use what you love and what you're good at to make a difference? You may not need to go to the other side of the world. God might need you to help someone down the block. Maybe it's time to use your energy to help a friend who is going through a difficult season of life. Maybe it's something you can do in your own home. Would you be bold enough to answer these questions honestly?

1. What are you good at doing? List everything that comes to mind.

2. What in your life, or in the lives of others, would you love to see changed?

3. What are you willing to do today to make that change? How can you use the talents God has given you to make a difference?

WRITE COOL STUFF HERE

WRITE COOL STUFF HERE

WRITE **COOL** STUFF HERE

CHAPTER 4

THE FRIENDSHIP

PRINCIPLE:
THE HOLY SPIRIT MAKES JESUS REAL IN US.

When I was in fourth grade, my family and I moved to a new town and I had to start at a new school. Now, you need to know something about me. When I was a boy, I was diagnosed with every learning disability imaginable. So they always sent me to the class where we wrote with those fat pencils and played with modeling clay all day. I was nervous about starting at the new school because, even as a boy, I knew that it wasn't easy making friends when you are seen clomping off of the short bus every day. I kept to myself and made no eye contact with anyone the morning of my first day. (Well, the eye contact part was because the very width and circumference of my eyes behind my glasses made it difficult for anyone to discern my general gaze. Look at your reflection in the back of a silver spoon and you will get the gist of what my glasses did to my face.) When I got to my classroom, the teacher instructed me to sit at a table beside a boy she said was named Bubba. Up until this point, I had never met a Bubba and thought they existed only in lame sitcoms about the South. But right there next to me was a real live Bubba.

Bubba and I became fast friends. Bubba could feel my pain about my glasses because he had a much more tragic social malady. I never really got the full story as to why, but Bubba had to screw in his teeth. He didn't have the luxury of wearing dentures or one of those retainer things with teeth attached. No, Bubba wasn't that lucky. Because of something that had to do with alignment, the poor guy had to twist his teeth into his head every morning and unscrew the bottom ones if he wanted to eat anything that required significant chewing. (And you thought it was bad when you couldn't get clear braces.) Bubba and I were something else to watch in the cafeteria. As he was unscrewing his teeth, I had to pull my glasses off so I could focus on my food up close. The problem was, due to my horrific eyesight, I had terrible hand-eye coordination and only about every fourth forkful actually made it into my mouth. And there was Bubba across from me just gumming away at his food while his teeth lay beside him on a napkin. As an adult, I can't imagine being seen in public eating like this, but Bubba and I were carefree. We knew we were different, but we had each other. Over that year at our little table in the corner with our fat pencils and Play-Doh, we got so close that we could finish each other's sentences.

I have met countless people since then and have a handful of really close friends, but there is nothing like those friends who knew you before you knew how to pretend everything was just dandy when it really wasn't. I always had terrible handwriting, but Bubba learned how to decipher it so that when he checked my papers, he could pretty much justify marking everything right. He was on my team. He was in my corner. Actually, I had a hard time finding my corner, so Bubba would nudge me toward it.

Have you ever been that close to another person — a friend who could unscrew his teeth in front of you, let his weaknesses show, and feel totally comfortable? Do you know the feeling of having a true friend?

Do you have a best friend, a BFF? If someone asked you to talk about your best friend, could you? Would you be able to share what makes that person special to you or what makes *the relationship unique? Your description wouldn't sound like a résumé or read like a profile page; it would be warm, passionate, and personal. You would be speaking from firsthand knowledge because you know your friend well.*

/ / / / / / / / / / / /

Knowing the Holy Spirit is not easy for a lot of people. It has been categorized as a topic that is weird, mystical, and scary. The life and work of the Holy Spirit cannot be summed up with a list of facts. The best way to know the Holy Spirit is to listen to someone who knows Him fully and is well acquainted with Him.

Jesus knew more about the Holy Spirit than anyone else. For Jesus this was *the* friendship. Jesus' life had been affected in every way by the work of the Holy Spirit. His birth was from the work of the Spirit. His ministry was anointed by the Spirit. Scripture says that at Jesus' baptism, He was full of the Holy Spirit. As Jesus began His ministry, He was anointed by the Spirit to fulfill prophecy, show God to others, and be an example for people to follow. He lived and worked in the power of the Spirit. He was led by the Spirit. He spoke in the authority of the Spirit. He acted on the power of the Spirit. He offered Himself as a sacrifice for sin by the energy of the Spirit.

> Jesus knew more about the Holy Spirit than anyone else. For Jesus this was *the* friendship.

He was resurrected by the power of the Spirit. The connection between Christ and the Spirit brings the believer into a living union with Jesus.

When Jesus spoke about the Spirit, He knew what He was talking about. John 14–16 records some of Jesus' final words to His disciples related to the presence and the work of the Holy Spirit. Notice the practical ways Jesus describes the work and the person of the Holy Spirit. Jesus makes it obvious that the Holy Spirit is not a weird force or ghost but rather Someone with whom you can have a relationship. The Holy Spirit is God. He is to be respected. He is not inferior to God but works to carry out His purpose. Because of the presence of the Spirit, God is not far away. Through the Spirit, all that is real about God is made real within us. This is why Jesus tells us that when He sends the Spirit into our lives, it is for our advantage.

 **PASSAGE:**
JOHN 16:7-15

> But I tell you the truth: It is for your good that I am going away. Unless I go away, the Counselor will not come to you; but if I go, I will send him to you. When he comes, he will convict the world of guilt in regard to sin and righteousness and judgment: in regard to sin, because men do not believe in me; in regard to righteousness, because I am going to the Father, where you can see me no longer; and in regard to judgment, because the prince of this world now stands condemned.
>
> I have much more to say to you, more than you can now bear. But when he, the Spirit of truth, comes, he will guide you into all truth. He will not speak on his own; he will speak only what he hears, and he will tell you what is yet to come. He will bring glory to me by taking from what is mine and making it known to you. All that belongs to the Father is mine. That is why I said the Spirit will take from what is mine and make it known to you.

In this passage, Jesus speaks of the personal ways the Holy Spirit works in our lives. The Holy Spirit makes us in character what we already are in Christ. The Spirit in our lives is in constant motion to convict, enable, repent, war against temptation, and apply forgiveness while making a way to deliver us from the worst of it. There are technical and theological terms for the works of the Spirit, but in this chapter they are placed in terms and phrases that are easily understandable – the way you might speak about a friend.

1. The Holy Spirit makes us feel the way God feels. Sometimes this isn't one of the happier works of the Spirit. The Holy Spirit shows us the way things really are. He unmasks our real character and makes us see the full weight of our choices and the consequences of living that way. When we feel the way God feels, that is called conviction. Conviction is the means by which the Spirit of God matures us by shining light on the hidden sin God wants deleted from our lives.

The conviction of the Spirit is not to drive us away from God but to draw us to God. The difference between conviction and condemnation is that condemnation produces guilt, shame, and the feeling of being unworthy to be in the presence of God. If what you are feeling is condemnation, you will not want to talk to God about it or spend time with Him. But if it's the Spirit, you will be willing to allow God's light to be shown on that area. If it's condemnation, it will make you want to hide. If it's conviction, you will be willing to deal with it. Where the Spirit of God deals with us, He always points us to Christ as the answer and gives us the assurance that we can be totally free from the things that have held us back.

> The Spirit in our lives is in constant motion to convict, enable, repent, war against temptation, and apply forgiveness while making a way to deliver us from the worst of it.

Because of the moral confusion of our world, many do not see their lives from any perspective other than their own. But when the Spirit begins to make us feel the way God feels in specific areas of our lives, we can be terribly awkward and uncomfortable. I once had someone say to me, "I think God is mad at me." I asked him why he thought so. He said, "This past weekend I went out and did the stuff I've always done on the weekends, and I felt terrible. I've never felt bad about doing that stuff before." I smiled, looked him straight in the eye, and said, "God's not mad at you. What you felt was conviction. That's one of the ways the Spirit of God ministers to you."

2. The Holy Spirit makes us compatible with God. The Holy Spirit removes everything that would kill our connection with God.

Further, the Spirit also applies the work of Jesus on the cross and His resurrection to our lives, which results in forgiveness and freedom. The Spirit makes the life of Christ real by dealing with our conduct and forgiving our sin. Where forgiveness and freedom collide, we experience life that is compatible with the life of God. This is the primary work of the Spirit. Before we received Jesus, we had a body and a soul. After we opened our lives to Jesus, the Spirit of God was placed inside of us. Our thoughts, desires, and actions can now be triggered from the Spirit of God living inside of us rather than just from our own sinful natures. Now we are a brand-new person, completed by the Spirit of God living on the inside of us.

> The Holy Spirit removes everything that would kill our connection with God.

3. The Holy Spirit gives us confidence in our faith. There are moments when we wonder what is true. We even wonder if our faith is real. It may be during circumstances that cause us to doubt, seasons of disappointment, or times when what we say with our lips and how we live our lives don't match up. But the Spirit tells us that our faith in Christ is real. In the worst of times, the presence of the Spirit confirms that Jesus is real and we are really His. God put His mark of the Spirit on us as a guarantee. Nothing can change that. His presence is forever. The permanence of His presence makes His power consistent in our lives.

4. The Holy Spirit gives us an ambitious assignment. Everybody wants to be known for doing something great. Whether it's for being on stage, throwing the biggest party, pulling off the most elaborate prank, we want to be remembered. All of those things, as cool as they are, last only for a moment. God has something for us to do that will impact eternity.

Our assignment is linked to the church. The church was not designed to be an organization or corporation of individuals who are concerned with only themselves. The church is made up of people who have been changed by the life, death, and resurrection of Jesus. The church has been brought together for one ambitious assignment: to share the message and work of Christ with the world. The Spirit-empowered church is the means by which the world will know Jesus, bringing all things under His leadership. This mission is accomplished as the church lives by the Spirit in truth, demonstrates mercy to the spiritual and physical needs of others, and speaks the life-changing power of Jesus. It is the Spirit who gives people the power to carry out this ambitious assignment. Your life is part of the strategy. The church needs you, and you need the church.

We need each other to accomplish the work God has designed us to do. Service in the kingdom of God is not a solo sport. By God's design, our talents are connected to the talents of others. The usefulness of these gifts grows only in the context of the church. Our talents are given to us for much more than our selfish purposes. They exist for God's building plan for the kingdom. The ambitious assignment that God has given us can only happen through the life of His church.

5. The Holy Spirit shows us talents we didn't know we had. We have all been given different talents. These are the things we are passionate about, in which we excel. But there is another dimension to our lives. Because of the work of the Spirit in us, we are given the gifts of the Spirit. These are the unique abilities and actions through which the Spirit is highlighted and the work of God is seen. These gifts are different from talents. These gifts often are supernatural downloads of motivation and ability for the purpose of doing God's work.

Spiritual gifts are how God chooses to make Himself seen in our lives. As we discover our spiritual skill set, we will be awakened to new interests we didn't know we had.

The Holy Spirit has a task to accomplish through each of us, and He places us as He sees fit. He also gifts us and empowers us as He accomplishes His work through us, giving us an active ministry. Have you found your gifts? Are you using them in a way that builds up the kingdom?

6. The Holy Spirit gives us the ability to reach out. To be a witness means to tell others how we have personally experienced Christ and what we have discovered in our relationship with Him. As witnesses, we get to see firsthand the work of Christ in our lives on a daily basis. When you hear the word *witness*, thoughts of preaching or yelling at someone probably come to mind. *Witness* means "genuine." Someone might say of a friend, "He's the real thing; he's a genuine person." That is to say that there is no doubt about who he is or what he believes. We are called to be witnesses, to be genuine in our expression of Jesus. Being the real thing spiritually is the work of the Spirit. Being a witness does not happen by adding formulas to arguments in order to prove a point. The Spirit creates the impulse and the know-how of being true and genuine in sharing the gospel.

> The Holy Spirit gives us the ability to be ready and real in the expression of our faith.

Being a genuine, consistent witness means that the bass line (to use a music metaphor) of the gospel is heard in all the parts of our lives. Through our words and our actions, we demonstrate that there is forgiveness of sin and that Jesus is reorienting our entire lives concerning all things spiritual, moral, and physical. The Holy Spirit gives us the ability to be ready and real in the expression of our faith. Talking about Jesus is not something we have to fear, because one of the promises of the Spirit is that we will be empowered to know what to speak, how to speak, and when to speak it. As witnesses, we then get to tell others what we've seen Jesus do in our lives and what we have heard in His Word. Nobody is out of His reach.

Jesus said that it was for our advantage that He would go away. He did this so the Spirit could be sent to us. God is for us and wants our lives to work. He is so committed to our success as Jesus followers that He sent His Spirit to ensure that everything that is commanded of us as believers would happen. As we follow the Spirit, He points us to Jesus and we are empowered to live the Spirit-filled life. Any believer committed to the Lordship of Jesus will experience the work of the Spirit.

⑦ UNPACKING THE PASSAGE

Take a moment to explore John 16:7-15 and answer these questions.

1. What is the Holy Spirit called in these verses?

2. According to this passage, what will the Holy Spirit do in our lives?

3. Put yourself in the place of one of the disciples. What would you have thought when you heard Jesus say that He was sending a Helper?

4. What are the advantages of knowing that the Holy Spirit lives within you?

👓 OFF THE PAGE

Sometimes when reading the Bible there is a tendency to flip open to the middle of a book and just start reading. When we start reading in the middle of a chapter or verse, it makes reading the Bible more difficult than it should be.

You can't read Scripture the way you watch TV. Pick a book of the Bible and start at the beginning of that book. Read an entire chapter in one sitting.

Reading a book of the Bible from beginning to end has a number of benefits:

- Prevents you from getting lost in the Bible
- Connects the themes of the Bible together
- Reveals Jesus
- Deepens your knowledge of Scripture
- Sharpens your skills to study
- Inspires you to live well
- Uncovers God's ongoing story line
- Reminds you that every page of Scripture is for your benefit
- Immerses you in the story and its characters
- Highlights the truths for you to consider

🔽 PERSONAL DOWNLOAD

Reread John 16:7-15, the chapter's passage. The following questions and suggestion for memorization will help you apply the principle of this chapter to your life and strengthen you in your journey toward being more like Christ.

1. Identify two areas in which you need the help of the Holy Spirit.

2. What is something you thought you could never do for God? How does knowing the Holy Spirit and how He works change your perspective?

3. How do you tell the difference between conviction and condemnation?

4. How would you explain the Holy Spirit to your friend?

5. Commit John 16:7 to memory. This verse will remind you that the Holy Spirit is always with you.

///

💬 LIVE THE WORD

A professor asked a question of his students that radically shifted their mindset and view of each other for the remainder of the semester. The question he posed to his students was "Are you going to remain pure before marriage, or will you be sexually involved before marriage?" The professor asked students to share their responses by walking to the left side to indicate they would be involved in a sexual relationship prior to marriage, or to the right side to indicate they wanted to remain pure for their future spouse. More than seventy students stood on the left side of the room, signifying they were going to be involved in a sexual relationship prior to marriage. On the right side of the room stood three individuals. That's right—only three individuals.

As the three individuals faced the majority of their classmates on the other side of the room, wondering what people might think and what would be said about them the next day, the professor said, "Now that you've chosen the direction you want to take, you have to defend your choice in somewhat of a debate fashion." These three individuals stood together knowing they would be called out. They faced the fire together, but they had more than just the three of them. God showed up with His Spirit and gave them the courage they needed to share their convictions. Not only did they stand together, they were able to celebrate together.

Go to www.firstbookchallenge.org to tell us your story about how God and His Word have made a difference in your life, friends, family, school, and church.

///

🔑 HEART CHALLENGE

Hearing this story may awaken within you memories, situations, or possibly even pain that you've encountered in your relationships with others when they discovered you were a follower of Christ.

1. Describe what you think the three students felt as they stood for what they believed.

2. Honestly and transparently tell which side of the room you would have been on.

3. Pray that God will give you the strength to carry the burdens of your convictions into the classroom and everywhere else you go. Ask Him for opportunities to live out your life according to His will and Word.

WRITE **COOL** STUFF HERE

WRITE COOL STUFF HERE ⟶

WRITE **COOL** STUFF HERE

CONCLUSION

Bringing the Spirit of God into our interaction with Scripture radically alters how we experience Scripture. When the Word and the Spirit are linked, our faith is stirred and our understanding of Scripture deepened. Because of the work of the Spirit, the Scripture that was revealed to the writers long ago comes to life in the one who reads it. The truth of Scripture becomes meaningful to us as we read. The words on the pages of Scripture are meant to be internalized. For this to happen, it requires the work of the Spirit. As we read, the Holy Spirit takes control of the historical works of God and connects His Word directly to the realities of our lives. Without question, the Word and the Spirit belong together.

The Bible functions in two primary ways: as a historical text filled with facts, events, and geography and as an instrument of the Spirit. In one way, we read the Bible. In another way, the Bible reads us. God's Word looks at the details of our lives and asks questions about our beliefs, choices, and destiny. The Word of God is at work in our lives. The Bible becomes the ground from which the Spirit speaks. Because of the work of the Spirit, the ancient works of the Scripture become fresh and new, inspiring us, stretching us, and igniting new possibilities in our lives. The Bible isn't a giant antique book resting on a coffee table. It is the God-breathed Word that gives life.

When the Word and the Spirit intersect in our lives, the truth is made real. The work of the Holy Spirit is essential for knowing the Word of God. For somebody who doesn't have a personal relationship with Jesus Christ, the Bible can be understood only historically. For the believer, because of the work of the Spirit, it becomes personal, living, and active. The Spirit brings to life the words God spoke long ago. Scripture becomes new and personal. The text becomes the living voice of God.

Shockingly, many Christians claim to respect Scripture but refuse to follow its teachings, instead picking and choosing only the parts they agree with and leaving the rest behind. There is one final ingredient to include in this discussion of encountering God's Word and His Spirit. That ingredient is *us*.

God initiates the truth through His Word and Spirit, but we have to be receptive. By the Holy Spirit, God makes Himself present to us and opens our eyes to understanding His Word. The role of the Holy Spirit is to make real the potential in our hearts and minds. The connection between the Word and the Spirit is vital to hearing and receiving His Word. The Bible is not a static collection of stories; rather, it orients us to God's unflinching truth. The Spirit enables us to enter into the Word and hear God speak to us.

As you hold your Bible, think about this: God has spoken and given us the foundation of Scripture. The Scripture is settled. We believe it to be God's Word. However, through the ministry of the Spirit, God is fully engaged in our lives and still communicating to us. He is never finished with changing the mind and the heart of the believer with His Word. The question is "How do the Spirit and the Word work together?" There are three specific ways the Spirit works in relation to Scripture.

1. The Holy Spirit helps us recognize the Word. Just reading the Bible academically will satisfy our intellectual longings, but it will not produce consistency unless faith is also present. There is a confidence the Spirit gives that cannot be obtained by simply understanding the evidence of Scripture. The Spirit enables us to hear the Word and receive it. The Spirit opens us up to an understanding of the Word that creates faith and helps us make decisions to live it out.

2. The Holy Spirit helps us interpret the Word. The role of the Spirit is crucial in interpreting the Bible. Every person knows what it's like to read the Bible and be bored to death while doing it. The Holy Spirit gives us spiritual discernment about what the Bible is saying. Without that discernment, there is no incentive to open the Bible or take it seriously. The truth of the text is not known only through historical reading or a word study. The goal is not to try to master the text but to place ourselves before the text and let the Spirit of God help us experience His Word. Being involved in the text of the Bible and having openness to its message puts us in a place where we can understand it. Reading the Bible can seem dry and pointless until the Holy Spirit gives us a creative breakthrough in understanding. We have an "aha moment." The truth of God and our circumstances connect and the Word makes sense. Where the Spirit of God is active, His truth is valued. The things that were written long ago are revealed anew to us.

3. The Holy Spirit helps us apply the Word. When the Spirit finds areas of our lives to work in, we must be sensitive to His leading. Often the application of the text is obvious: love one another, worship God, believe His promises. The Spirit brings into effect the Word of God to specific situations in our lives. The Spirit was given to lead us into truth and apply Jesus' words in our lives.

Encountering the Holy Spirit pulls us out of apathy by giving us a new momentum by which to live and brings us into an adventurous life being led by the Spirit of the living God!

BE A BETTER BIBLE READER

1. As you read Scripture, make a mental picture of what is going on in the text.
2. Highlight verses, words, and phrases that stand out to you. Often these serve as indicators that the Spirit of God wants to speak to you about these things.
3. Every time you eat or drink, make a point to look at the verse you read earlier that day. This is where technology, sticky notes, and note cards come in handy.
4. Work what you've read into a conversation with others, perhaps by restating the verse. You might say, "I read something about that the other day." Talking about what you have read will make you recall it, which will help you learn it.
5. Approach Scripture with a flexible mind and an open heart. Don't assume you know everything about what you are preparing to read. As you read God's Word, you'll realize how much more you need to know.
6. Read Scripture to encounter God. Let the verses lead you to a deeper insight than you could experience on your own.
7. Read Scripture every day. The depth of your experience will be in direct proportion to the amount of attention you give God's Word. There is no substitute for reading Scripture. Use online resources such as Bible dictionaries, commentaries, and encyclopedias. Remember that although these tools can assist you in your understanding of Scripture, there is nothing that can take the place of reading it.
8. Write down questions you have after reading God's Word. Next time you read Scripture, these questions will lead you to what you are looking for.

9. Don't be afraid to take on big topics in Scripture such as sin, suffering, and the uniqueness of the deity of Christ. Have confidence that as you study His Word, God will speak to you.

10. Remember that you need the Spirit's help when reading the Bible. Reading without the Spirit's help won't do much for you. It's God's Spirit that shapes your character and your service to others.

11. Restate the verses as a status update — 140 characters or less. Distilling a verse down to Twitter-sized chunks helps clarify the meaning so you can carry it with you.

PASSING ON THE FIRST BOOK CHALLENGE:

CARRY IT. LIVE IT. GIVE IT.

You can be a great Christian – if you are willing to pay the price. To pursue greatness in Christianity means to be willing to turn your life of faith into an intentional pursuit. Being intentional means making choices based on God and the priority of His Word. Living your faith on purpose means that you begin to let the relationship you have with God and the knowledge of His Word influence all your decisions and your relationships with others. Being intentional means you've decided it's worth it to invest in your spiritual life as well as help others with their spiritual lives.

Inside every person is a great believer waiting to be unleashed. Most students have found that they make more progress as a disciple when helping someone else do the same. Investing spiritually in the lives of others is an amazing experience. Now that you have journeyed through this phase of the First Book Challenge – learning skills for reading and recalling the Word and having a deeper understanding of what a Spirit-led life looks like – take the First Book pledge.

THE FIRST BOOK PLEDGE

You have completed your journey through this phase of the First Book Challenge, but your journey is not over. Your relationship with God continues to grow. Take the First Book Challenge a step further:

- Be a change agent on your campus.
- Lead at least one person through these four sessions.
- Carry your Bible with you every day.
- Be intentional about how you live.
- Give one of your friends a Bible.

Will you take the First Book Challenge? Sign your name below to indicate that you pledge to make God's Word the first book you turn to in your life.

_____

signature   date

You are wired to make a difference. Whenever God's Book becomes the First Book, great things happen! You can find additional resources for First Book Challenge at www.firstbookchallenge.org.

ABOUT THE AUTHORS

DAVID EDWARDS has launched seven citywide, multi-church Bible studies for high school students, which have ranged in attendance from 200 to 1,600. He is a friend of the local church and pastors and is a supporter of Intelligent Youth Ministry.

David connects Scripture to students and their culture while helping leaders and parents connect to the next generation. He masterfully applies biblical truths to current issues in an honest, humorous, and understandable form. His mission is to reintroduce the truth of God's Word by meeting people where they are in life and bringing them one step closer to knowing and becoming like Jesus Christ.

David has authored nineteen books. He travels and speaks more than three hundred times a year for churches, camps, retreats, and leadership meetings. For more information, connect with David at DaveTown.com.

JOHN STAMPER speaks and writes nationally to audiences of all ages. However, he has a special heart to see students rise up and take a leadership role in their families, schools, and churches. Over the past fifteen years, John has been dedicated as a pastor to teaching, discipling, and mentoring students and families through churches, schools, camps, sporting events, and community organizations. He has the unique ability to connect with all ages, enlightening and motivating individuals to follow Christ and connect to His Word. For more information, connect with John at johnstamper.info.

Other books in the
First Book Challenge series!

The Message: First Book Challenge Edition
Eugene H. Peterson

You're learning how to read and study the Bible — why not learn to understand it better with *The Message*? Written in contemporary language, the way you speak to a friend, *The Message* is easy to read and understand for any age.

978-1-61747-833-8

VAST
978-1-61521-914-8

ALIVE
978-1-61747-166-7

MY LIFE IS **TOUGHER** THAN MOST **PEOPLE REALIZE.**

I TRY TO
KEEP EVERYTHING
IN BALANCE:
FRIENDS, FAMILY, WORK,
SCHOOL, AND GOD.

IT'S NOT EASY.

I KNOW WHAT MY
PARENTS BELIEVE AND
WHAT MY PASTOR SAYS.

BUT IT'S NOT
ABOUT THEM.
IT'S ABOUT ME...

ISN'T IT TIME I
OWN MY FAITH?

THROUGH THICK AND THIN, KEEP YOUR HEARTS AT ATTENTION, IN
ADORATION BEFORE CHRIST, YOUR MASTER. BE READY TO SPEAK
UP AND TELL ANYONE WHO ASKS WHY YOU'RE LIVING THE WAY
YOU ARE, AND ALWAYS WITH THE UTMOST COURTESY. 1 PETER 3:15 (MSG)

www.navpress.com | 1-800-366-7788   TH1NK by NAVPRESS

PERFECT for **Wednesday nights** or **weekend retreats**!

JUSTLIKECHRIST
GET EVERYTHING YOU NEED WITH THESE BOX SETS.

∨
∨ Full of vibrant, colorful pages, these four-week studies are filled with dynamic group activities, Bible study questions, and a memory verse each week for students. Each box contains 10 student books, a DVD, and a Web license (includes your teaching lessons).

∨
∨ These pocket-sized devotional journals help students engage in God's Word day by day.

[
JustLikeChrist studies allow students to dig deeper in God's Word and relate the Bible to real life. Teachers and leaders access the lessons through an online delivery system.
]

FOR MORE INFORMATION, call **1-888-811-9934**
or go online to **JustLikeChrist.com**.

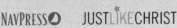

The Message Means Understanding

Bringing the Bible to all ages

*T*he *Message* is written in contemporary language that is much like talking with a good friend. When paired with your favorite Bible study, *The Message* will deliver a reading experience that is reliable, energetic, and amazingly fresh.

To find *The Message* that is right for you, go to **www.navpress.com** or call **1-800-366-7788**.

NAVPRESS
Discipleship Inside Out™

HELPING STUDENTS
KNOW CHRIST
THROUGH
HIS WORD

What will YOUR STUDENTS do this summer?

Choose from TWO great options.

STUDENT LIFE CAMP

- Engaging worship from experienced worship leaders
- Learning through sound biblical teaching and Bible study
- Community in family groups
- Freedom for you to focus on your students

STUDENT LIFE MISSION CAMP

- Repairing homes, landscaping, painting, and other work projects
- Serving food, organizing donations, and helping at homeless shelters
- Visiting nursing homes and mental health centers
- Leading children's activities and teaching Bible stories to children

For more information on Student Life Camps and Mission Camps, go to **studentlife.com** or call **1-800-718-2267**.